I0415586

TRANSCENDIA

TRANSCENDIAN PASSPORT

The bearer has chosen to present themselves as a member citizen of Transcendia, the country, company and work of art. I am glad they have chosen to use the Transcendian Passport and desire that you as authorized to protect your border show them honor and passage as you desire of Transcendia and its authorized defenders.

Should any problem, question, crisis or danger to the liberty or wellbeing either by accident or on purpose arise limiting the liberty or wellbeing of the Transcendian here before you, please inform Transcendia the best method.
Telephone Russell Scott Day
1+919-960-8446
I would perfer messages via the contact on Transcendia.org

Russell Scott Day

_____
Founder of Transcendia

(There exist about 300 prior hand made passports I signed and numbered. Those were given out of my hand, and are obviously more valuable.)

Insert picture.

Name_____

_____

_____

Date of

issuance._____

Date of
Birth_____
Place of
Birth_____

_____

_____

Citizenship_____

_____

Citizenship of origin

_____

_____

Certifications of importance such as Pilot License, Drivers License, or other certifications such as Engineering Credentials or Diplomatic standing such as Ambassador, Prime Minister, or Premier.

Entrance

Exit

Entrance

Exit

Entrance

Exit

Entrance

Exit

Entrance

Exit

Entrance

Exit

Entrance

Exit

Entrance

Exit

Entrance

Exit

Entrance

Exit

Entrance

Exit

Entrance

Exit

Entrance

Exit

Entrance

Exit

Entrance

Exit

Entrance

Exit

Entrance

Exit

Entrance

Exit

Entrance

Exit

Entrance

Exit

Entrance

Exit

Entrance

Exit

Entrance

Exit

Entrance

Exit

Entrance

Exit

Entrance

Exit

Entrance

Exit

Entrance

Exit

Entrance

Exit

Entrance

Exit

Entrance

Exit

Entrance

Exit

It recommended that travelers get inoculations against as many diseases as their doctor suggests. It is good practice to see a doctor before periods of travel.
Many practiced travelers drink the same brand of bottled water wherever they go.

I see in my US Passport 404-332-4559 as a health advisory number to call.

Because water is your most assured interaction with any locality, pay attention to what you drink, and use purification tablets or bottles that perform that work.

Whatever insurance for your health travels the most with you is recommended. Transcendian Whole Life Citizenship Insurance is a future aim.

The US requires that you report cash carriage of 10,000 dollars, which is a low amount for some pilots who may need to pay cash for fuel in some situations.

I suggest you are prepared by your offices for fuel purchases and consider tankering as an alternative to purchasing fuel. However if you must buy fuel where cash is required, do so from as reputable a supplier as possible.

I highly recommend employing a mechanic when flying in unfamiliar and dangerous nations with full awareness that fuel handing best practices may not be understood in some locations.

Plus things break.

Transcendian Notes

I am working to make it so that you can simply buy this passport, and encourage you to do so. It is a good practice to have more than one passport.
Citizenship in Transcendia will be by nature voluntary and new.

My personal destiny mandated that I do what I can to prevent atomic war, which is now best called Apocalyptic Riot.

I moved from Godwin Anarchy to Westminster Parliamentary Governance, with a strong dependence on Roberts Rules of Order.

Godwin Anarchy dictates that there are two main responsibilities of any government. Those are Defense and Education.

Those are government responsibility constants. In any government large and small, from town to metropolis to multi-million nation defense of the poor, rich and in between is required.

Taxes paid however are to not ever ignore Defense and Education in all its forms, meaning pure water to border enforcement with arms, schools to signage.

Education enables us to live less complicated lives with a complicated understanding of life which is uncomplicated if you have the necessary skills, which take some focus.

We are more likely to focus on learning with our friends.   I highly recommend peer to peer learning practices.

Transcendia will create and operate schools and universities that award peer awarded certifications as are awarded pilot certificates.

Best practice degrees will be honored when such certifications do not apply.

Transcendia will join with other nations if it fits with the highest ideals of ethical behavior in actions as may be possible, in the pursuit of safety and peace.

When it is impossible to keep peace with the neighbors inside as the airport operates according to its own port laws and customs, it will be best for Transcendia and Transcendians to simply give up and leave.

Transcendian Public Relations are based on ethics and we get a good start and some bit of a pass because we don't really have a history of hypocrisy. We want to avoid creating a greed based operation.

You may be greedy for Strength, Wisdom, Beauty, and Humor? Things that start well are more likely to end well.

We could very well start off without having a war, and some limitations on our defensive actions could mean a 3 D War movie would give us a good budget for everyone to be armed individually properly for airport defense.

A spiritual practice I developed because I wanted to write a book for the Bible is to throw the I Ching to a specific question, and read the Reading for the Day in the Bible. It combines the two different senses of time, Fate and Fiat, Choice and Chance, and I have found it works well for me.

Boredom and Bliss in alternation worked to create in me a vision.

If you haven't had any spiritual experiences of your own, we all work well together when we just do what is ethical, since some things called moral, aren't ethical.

Working *With* others is the way. Owning others is not the way.

Our leaders are to understand and be passionate in their understanding of the Transcendian goals of moderating world economic crises.

Obviously physical banks on all Transcenidian airports using Insurodollars will help those who use money to create, buy, and sell. Money stockpiled at too great an amount with no purpose and producing payout unearned via accounting fictions is not approved.

"It isn't how much money you have, but what you do with it that matters." (I said this to my first wife when she was spending money to divorce me in alarming ways. Steve Forbes is also credited with this quote.)

Corruption and war Keep people poor. We don't want people to be poor. It creates safety hazards when people are made poor.

Pot and other vices will be legal as they are common to ports with tolerant government and sensible taxation on transactions. We may as well look to Las Vegas for best practices regarding community peace where excitement is a great deal of the product.

Taxes on Transactions, are all that is practical for a port nation where some ships don't dock again for reasons beyond our control, or desire to control.

Control your own mind and your own and protect your own and we will be honorable towards you as you are towards us.

Hard drugs and powerful hallucinogens must be controlled for purity and those interested in using them need to be aware that these drugs do not make you feel normal, or leave you normal. The deaths that occur, do often come not from the use of the drug, but from unknowns and contaminations. Pain control drugs are not fun to withdraw from and misuse means eventual nausea or otherwise sad complications.

Marijuana will be legal for pilots, though flying high will not be.

Eating pot and hashish will mean you cannot legally operate a plane for 3 days.

Smoking pot or hashish will mean operation is illegal for 24 hours for Professional Commercial Charter, and Private pilots. (Smoking is the same as vaporization in this context.)

The goal of Transcendia is to operate a network of culturally neutral airports (ports) under the one Transcendian Flag using Parliamentary Democracy and Roberts Rules of Order in meetings where and when laws are determined and projects allocated fungible assets.

Nothing works if you don't believe in it.

We will as a nation work to eliminate Weapons of Mass Destruction and at the least prevent the smuggling and use of such weapons.

Transcendia intends to use the INSURODOLLAR, which is pooled equity from whole life policies for all Transcendian citizens joined in and later gaining citizenship when birthed by Transcendian citizens.

Purchase of a Transcendian Passport will help move Transcendia towards a reality. Bulk purchases to be systematically distributed to people in need of identification and travel papers is desirable as long as one person in *the line* will vouch for others.

It is obvious that unregulated use of the Transcendian Passport will diminish the value of the document, and that therefore a side work of bureaucratica for station agents of airport and port employ in the distribution of Transcendian Passports is desirable.

It cannot claim to be a real nation now because it has not even the resources of the American Automobile Association that sends an attorney if you get arrested on the road driving.

A real nation has an army.

Transcendians will on the airports where they live and work all be required to be armed to the best of their capabilities.
Some people cannot carry firearms because they don't like them and don't want to learn how to operate them. They will be required to carry pepperspray, and other non lethal weapons when performing public and office duties on and for Transcendian ports, depots and airports.

Transcendia will use the Napoleonic Siege Strategy of one circle looking in and one looking out for threats against the airport and its people.

In correspondence with Andre`
Lewin Chairman of the French UN
Association I worked to advance
the power of United Nations
Television in hopes of using more
truthful news and information to
cut back on wars that come from
Mass Mind Control, Public
Relations ploys, and Propaganda.

We need still to advance a more
accessible and better United
Nations Television. Transcendia
will produce and distribute its own
television channel aimed at
Education and entertainment as
the mental landscape demands.
Obviously a nation of ports and
airports will need Weather
Channel sorts of programing.

I volunteered Transcendia as an Exile Island option so that national leaders who are in the position of needing to flee their positions, for whatever reasons, have a way out.

Transcendia as a nation that will have airports will do whatever is within it's power to fill in for those failures of the United Nations and work with best practice organizations we cannot live without, such as the World Health Organization, or the International Civil Aviation Organization.

7/19/2014

Russell Scott Day

You may print out and fill out this application as it exists right now and mail it to:

Russell Scott Day
301 Pleasant Dr.
Carrboro, NC 2750

Application for a Transcendian Passport

Date_____

Name_____
____

Age, date of birth____ _____

Telephone email and other addresses you would like to provide for reference, rescue, or relay.

Temporary
address_____

_____

Permanent
address_____

_____
_____
_____

What does Citizenship in Transcendia mean to you?

_____
_____
_____
_____
_____

Have you Read the letters etc., or do you know the Founder?

Internet Archives may help you find earlier works written on The Refrigerator.net, and popwars.com under the column name Transcendia War Commentary. Currently the most going Transcendia website is Transcendia.org/wordpress. UNTV was the main work of Transcendia.org, first edition. The Transcendia.wikidot.com was put together by the volunteer Garth Hoyman, and is very valuable to be used holding still the original passport.

Are you a Pilot Captain, Ship Captain, Astronaut, or Cosmonaut?____

_____

_____

If so how many hours and what certifications do you have? _____

Have you ever launched a model or real rocket?

_____

_____

Who are your Heroes and Why?

_____

_____

_____

_____

How do you perceive the statement, "We are not here, to figure out, how not to do it."?

_____

_____

_____

_____

What is your favorite poem or poet?

_____

_____

Were you ever a Boy Scout, or a Girl Scout?

_____

What do you think of the idea of making a Virtual

Reality War Movie that would replace a real war in order to found Transcendia through ticket sales?

_____
_____
_____
_____

What imaginary future war do you think of for a good movie?

_____
_____
_____
_____

Do you think Transcendia should buy airports, or lease them?

_____

Do you think Transcendia should employ the United Nations Peacekeeping Force in leiu of creating its own Army, or Peace Keeping Force?

_____
_____
_____
_____

I have decided that Transcendia needs to have its own army if you consider Haiti. Some warrior professionals are born to a destiny of violence, and Transcendia needs to have people willing and wise to suffer this unique work in the open and in the dark._____

_____
_____
_____

What is the difference between Character, and Personality? _____

_____

(Personality does not change, but character can. -Founders belief from watching seagulls.) What does Vision, Usurpation, and Inheritance have to do with the way the world is?

_____
_____
_____
_____

What is a Pro Active Civil Demonstration? Transcendia has used the Message Rocket and imagines the high speed flower bombing, and wants to know of more in line with such heroic demostrations of power and wisdom.

_____
_____
_____
_____

How is that different from Civil Disobedience?

_____
_____
_____
_____

Do you value your life? _____

Do you have children? _____

Do you want to have children? _____

What will it take to make the world better for your children, than it has been for you?_____
_____
_____
_____

Is Transcendia a part of that?_____

www.ingramcontent.com/pod-product-compliance
Lightning Source LLC
Chambersburg PA
CBHW070839290526
45795CB00002B/920

* 9 7 8 1 4 9 1 0 8 8 4 1 8 *